THE NEW PARADIGM

IN BUSINESS, MARKETING AND CAREER

10 BESTSELLING BOOKS REVIEWED BY PIERRE F. WALTER

ILLUSTRATED EDITION

Tom Butler-Bowden

Laurence G. Boldt

Edward de Bono

Sergio Zyman

Published by Sirius-C Media Galaxy LLC

http://sirius-c-publishing.com

http://siriuscmedia.com

http://ipublica.com

ISBN 978-1-468145-12-0

Contact Information Pierre F. Walter

publisher@sirius-c-publishing.com

About Pierre F. Walter

http://drpfw.info

Quotation Suggestion

Pierre F. Walter, *The New Paradigm in Business, Marketing and Career: 10 Bestselling Books Reviewed,* Newark: Sirius-C Media Galaxy LLC, 2010

About the Author

Pierre F. Walter is an international lawyer, researcher, author and lecturer. After finalizing his studies in German law and European integration with diplomas in both disciplines in 1982, he graduated in December 1987 at the law faculty of the University of Geneva as *Docteur en Droit* in international law. The doctorate was funded by scholarships from the *Swiss Institute of Comparative Law*, Lausanne, and from the *University of Geneva*, as well as a Fulbright Travel Grant for an assistantship with Professor Louis B. Sohn at UGA Law School Department of International Law, Athens, Georgia, USA, in 1985. Pierre F. Walter also served as a research assistant to Freshfields, Bruckhaus, Deringer, Cologne, Germany in 1983 and to Lalive Lawyers, Geneva, in 1987.

Pierre F. Walter writes, lectures and teaches in English, German and French languages; he has written *more than ten thousand pages* embracing all literary genres, including *novels, short stories, film scripts, essays, selfhelp books, monographs* and extended *book reviews*. Also a pianist and composer, he has realized 40 CDs with jazz, newage and relaxation music.

Pierre F. Walter's professional publications span the domains *International Law, Criminal Law, Holistic Science, Psychology, Education, Shamanism, Ecology, Spirituality, Quantum Physics, Systems Theory, Natural Healing, Peace Research, Personal Growth, Selfhelp* and *Consciousness Research*.

110 Book Reviews, thirty-eight audio books and more than hundred video lectures were realized in the years 2005-2010. Besides, Pierre F. Walter is editor of a series 'Great Minds', which features scientists, artists and authors of genius from Leonardo to Fritjof Capra. In his 2011 series of scholarly articles, the author treats various topics from the realms of social science, psychology, mythology, medicine, oriental wisdom and psychoanalysis. In addition, in 2011, Pierre F. Walter published specially targeted readers, book reviews, on the New Paradigm in Business, Marketing and Career, and in Science and Systems Theory, as well as in Consciousness, Psychology, Healing and Spirituality.

Pierre F. Walter publishes via his Delaware firm *Sirius-C Media Galaxy LLC* and the imprints IPUBLICA and Sirius-C Media (SCM).

For Nelson, in gratitude

CONTENTS

For many who came to me seeking career guidance, a better job (as defined by pay and benefits alone) was not enough. There was a real desire for a broader conception of work – one that would reflect the spiritual as well as the material life of man. My search for such a vision of work let me finally to the notion of work as art, the unique creative expression of the individual.

– Laurence G. Boldt, Zen and the Art of Making a Living (1993), p. xii

LAURENCE G. BOLDT

Laurence G. Boldt is a writer and career consultant based in the San Francisco bay area. Boldt is highly versed in Oriental wisdom and especially *Zen*, and his books are all beautifully designed and edited, with a true abundance of quotes from wisdom books, and Zen graphics. I have been immensely enriched and blessed by Boldt's profound practical and spiritual wisdom and I do not presently now any career coach who can tip even remotely at the expertise and holistic insights of this great human and prolific author. I can whole-heartedly recommend and endorse each of his various books.

His main publications are *Zen and the Art of Making a Living: A Practical Guide to Creative Career Design*, New York: Penguin Arkana, 1993; *How to Find the Work You Love*, New York: Penguin Arkana, 1996; *Zen Soup: Tasty Morsels of Zen Wisdom From Great Minds East & West*, New York: Penguin Arkana, 1997; *The Tao of Abundance: Eight Ancient Principles For Abundant Living*, New York: Penguin Arkana, 1999.

Laurence G. Boldt

Zen and the Art of Making a Living

A Practical Guide to Creative Career Design
New York: Penguin Arkana, 1993
New and Updated Edition, 1999
(Quotes are from the Original Edition)

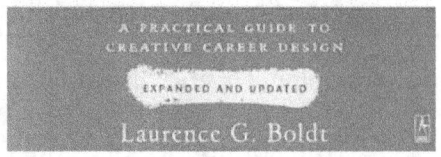

Zen or the Art of Making a Living

is a highly useful career guide, and

at the same time much more than a

career guide. Laurence G. Boldt is

not just an excellent career coach, but a wise man. His years of studying

Zen and Taoism have done their traces in this extraordinary book that is

not comparable with anything similar on the whole of the American and

European coach-products market. This book is not just a book - it's an

art work. And my congratulations expand from the author to the pub-

lisher. I have read many books in my life, and I am myself the publisher

of all my works, thus I know about layout, design and style. I have been

disappointed over the last years with some of the multinational pub-

lishers, and found typos even in the books of Deepak Chopra. However,

Penguin did an excellent editing, and they seem to comply with an ex-

cellent standard in just everything they do. This book is an example for

that, and I haven't found one single spelling or style error in it.

Myself being a coach, I can particularly evaluate and appreciate the in-

credible amount of work, and of wisdom, that Boldt put in this book. It's

Published by Sirius-C Media Galaxy LLC, 2011

one of my most cherished books in the library. I have read it twice, entirely, and the first read included filling out almost all worksheets, and still sometimes just look through it to read quotes or see the wonderful reproductions of Japanese and Chinese ink art, calligraphy and Zen motifs.

I have long thought about books and book prices over the last twenty years, and I can only wonder why the best books, the books that are the most valuable, precious, and extraordinary are always very modestly priced. There are design books on the market that assemble ink spots and sell for 150$ each, and a book like the present one that can serve you for about ten years without being outdated for the least, comes with such a modest price tag, despite the richness of its content. This truly is excellent publishing strategy! This is how it should to make the best accessible to virtually everybody, and even students. And this book is for young people, and all those who have kept a *beginner's mind* as it is put in Zen.

Let me offer some more flesh in this review, commenting on a few quotes from the text, so that you can learn appreciating the style Boldt writes in, a style that I myself find easy to read, and yet that a much younger friend of mine from San Francisco finds *way above the usual*. I guess what puts him off is the Tao philosophy that virtually interpenetrates all of Boldt's books. I am myself a Western Taoist, so for me this book really speaks *my language*, as it were, and for those who are still untouched by the wisdom traditions of the world, I can only say this:

– Boys and girls, please don't blame the author for your ignorance. Once you have done your spiritual quest similar to his, you will write in a very similar style, and what you now appreciate most in your cultural and social setting will lose a lot of its importance!

The centerpoint, to begin with, in Boldt's art of career coaching is his redefinition of *work as art*. He writes at the very start of the book:

Laurence G. Boldt
For many who came to me seeking career guidance, a better job (as defined by pay and benefits alone) was not enough. There was a real desire for a broader conception of work – one that would reflect the spiritual as well as the material life of man. My search for such a vision of work let me finally to the notion of work as art, the unique creative expression of the individual./xii

And indeed, the young friend I mentioned above who found Boldt's vision *above the head* is one of those young men who do a money job and find both the job and the rest of their lives absolutely *standard*. What this book is about is that: life, work, love, relationships - and energy! The energy input namely that lifts you out of a standard life and triggers your quantum leap in a first-hand life. Without energy input, you won't create anything worthwhile in either of these fields. What does that mean, energy input? It means vision, dedication, commitment and persistence.

Published by Sirius-C Media Galaxy LLC, 2011

Very modestly so, Boldt refers to his book as a *transition resource book*, but I can testify that it's much much more than that:

> **Laurence G. Boldt**
> This book is, of course, a transition resource book and hardly the last word. It provides a technology for applying a love-inspired orientation toward work within the existing economic, educational, and social structures. We might add that these structures do not, for the most part, encourage one to be oneself to serve one's fellow man in a spirit of love and beauty./xiv

The important detail in this quote is that Boldt speak of a *love-inspired* orientation toward work, and here we get to the core of his message. It shows the reader right at the start that this work is not one of those self-help manuals with their quick fixes 'for getting a job'; actually, none of Boldt's books is a quick fix manual - fortunately so. Boldt rightly states that when you just want a job that pays your bills, your are living with a bottomline paradigm that will lead you nowhere. Where there is no vision, the people perish, says the Bible.

> **Laurence G. Boldt**
> Yet, if we are not builders, if our dreams are not given the shape, form, and substance of living reality, then they are nothing more than phantoms and platitudes, the mirages we chase to escape a world we are unwilling to confront and love. The true idealist is no dewy-eyed dreamer, but a committed foot soldier in the cause of his vision./xxii

Ego-bound living with its limitations is one of the core issues for being jobless, or for creeping along in a pay-job over decades. And what is ego? Let us be careful with jumping to a definition, for it's not that easy. Let's try to approach the question by asking what is *not* ego. Can we say that true love, and the passion to do something we love, we truly love to engage in, is not ego? I think most people would agree with that. Boldt metaphorically depicts the ego as the 'little king' in us:

> **Laurence G. Boldt**
> We were promised that we would be little kings, and yet it seems we have so little control over the direction of our lives. The little king is a prisoner of his own freedom – from responsibility and conscience. His inner life is barren and hollow; his humanity, atrophied; his creativity, flat./xxxiii

Most of our well-to-do consumer children indeed are treated like little princes and princesses; spoiling children is not very conducive to bringing out the best in a human. We want to face reality, not standard reality. Children want to grow in autonomy, and not in entanglement with their parents and educators. The more we police children and keep them in cocoons of plastic and lies, the more we infantilize them, the more we render them truly inapt for mastering their lives.

All is set and setting in life, and especially work. All work is imbedded in a culture, and to work in San Francisco is not the same as working in Bangkok or Rome, and it requires different attitudes and experiences. On the other hand, it's true that international lifestyle standardizes job expectations more and more, and that we are gradually heading into a

Published by Sirius-C Media Galaxy LLC, 2011

globalized job environment. In this overall grasp of the globe by the international business culture, some values may get lost. Boldt writes:

Laurence G. Boldt
Today, even art has become commercialized. It has become a tool for profit and, therefore, a means for better controlling the environment, rather than the revelation of deep inner experience./xxxvii

There is a spiritual quest to be felt throughout the book, expressed by the author appealing to his audience to be cautious with applying standard values or consumer values to their lives, and rather put the focus on our inner life, our individual values, and our special gifts and talents. He writes:

Laurence G. Boldt
You are to depend on society for its evaluation of your sanity – measured, not in terms of the ancient wisdom or sacred psychologies, but in terms of normality – the sharing of the society-dominant world view./xliv

That author means that when you want to survive as an individual in a highly labeling society, you must not look at normalcy, but in the contrary at what is not normal, what is unusual, what is exceptional, what is extra-ordinary in the real sense of the word: outside of the ordinary. And you have to mold your self-vision accordingly, because if you envision yourself as an 'in-fitter', you are done. Boldt's cultural criticism is not a per-se item in the book but it serves to open our critical mind so that we are able to build true autonomy, that we become self-reliant. He writes:

Laurence G. Boldt

The Roman Catholic tradition epitomizes the king model. Early Roman Catholic churches were called Basilicas, or royal houses. The Pope wears a crown and carries a staff; you kneel to kiss his ring. I once saw the Pope entering Saint Peter's at the Vatican. There he was with all his attendants – being carried slowly down the aisle on a palanquin – the Swiss Guards standing sharply at attention. When at last he sat upon the throne, the entire congregation broke into applause. This is a king. The Pope standing in for King God. The accent in this model is on authority and decrees issues from on high./lii

This is not just ridiculous. It *is* ridiculous, but it is taken for serious, and television screens all over the world, virtually every day, display similar pictures. These images are mediatized and become almost archetypal, and for the least they become models of behavior, and they are part of our collective unconscious. The rub is that if you are driven by them, you are done. And you are not going to be liberated from them by declaring that religion has *no value* for you, but only if you take the time and effort to really make out your place, your stance, your position with regard to religion, with regard to hierarchies, with regard to authority. You have to get involved with that, deep inside of you, and see what is true for you, and what is not. Otherwise, if you just brush over all this, like most people do, you will be a religion-addict without even aware of it, in the sense that you just follow authority. But because you are playing hide-

Published by Sirius-C Media Galaxy LLC, 2011

and-seek with yourself, you remain shallow, disinterested, uncommitted, scant and superficial. And if you are like most people, you will not get to work the work you love and love the love you cherish. So your distinction must come prior to your job search, it must come from the whole of your being, and not just your so-called 'professional life', which is a mask, just like other masks we are all wearing.

Now, what does it mean to look at life the way non-ordinary people look at life? Boldt gives a hint, and his example really is well-put:

Laurence G. Boldt

To describe Michelangelo's David as a marble statue of a Hebrew king in his youth gives you the facts, but none of the spirit or emotional power of the work. To say that Don Quixote is the story of a madman wandering about in hallucination strips it of the power, spirit, and art of its message. It is no less ridiculous to reduce your life to a set of facts. You are not your place of birth, your height, weight, or degrees, your résumé, or credit history. You are a being of spirit, emotional power, and intelligence./6

Boldt has a wonderful sense of humor and that makes reading this book such an adventure! To look at art as a soul experience, and from a soul perspective, and not from a material, object-centered perspective is where the difference is. Boldt explains:

Laurence G. Boldt

Many today would have us believe that art is for the cultured few – the museum hounds and the wine and cheese set. The implication is that art is too good to be contaminated with the vulgar business of living. While art is safely locked away from the soiling hands of the common man, the greatest vulgarity of all is perpetuated. Art is reduced to an investment commodity. In the name of protection (from the masses), art has become a favorite form of capital speculation./37

When we see how what could be called the *business worldview* distorts the very meaning of life, and especially of art, we get a feel for taking care of our real values, instead of selling ourselves for a fake value, and thus way under price. When you develop the perspective of looking at yourself as a precious and unique individual, you will probably stop taking your life as an assembler-machine of labels put on it by society, and you will begin to ponder about what is unique in you, within you, and about you. And then, Boldt says, you become a hero, but only then, after your have shifted your perspective or self-vision:

Laurence G. Boldt
The Hero decides from himself what to focus his attention on (what is important), and in so doing, what the story of his life will be about./50

When you decide for yourself instead of leaving it up to society to decide for you, you take charge of your life, you become response-able for your living experience and all that it involves, including your love life. Work and love, love and work, are one unit. Boldt emphasizes this over and over in this and other of his books. Love is not that big word without meaning our media suggest us it were; in the contrary is it no word, but simply *pure meaning*. Does your work have meaning for you? Before

Published by Sirius-C Media Galaxy LLC, 2011

this can happen, Boldt says, you have to begin asking questions, and not let society ask the questions *for you*. It's by asking questions that you get answers, not by taking over answers from others:

> **Laurence G. Boldt**
> What distinguishes the hero from the rest is that he or she chooses the questions and earnestly seeks them; the rest blindly, and often half-heartedly, follow the conventional questions of their society./91

I shall stop here with this rather long review, but not without mentioning that for Boldt imagination is a very important ingredient in the toolbox you need to build for realizing a meaningful career. Imagination is not very much stressed as a value in our present educational system, and so we are called upon to develop it against the stream, so to speak, or by recovering our inner child of the past, that surely was full of imagination:

> **Laurence G. Boldt**
> Contemplating – seeing through the game – allows you to reclaim your imaginative power. You are free to use your imagination to build a life born out of the impulses of your own creative center. You put your faith in your creative intuitions and capacities rather than in the hope of some future reward or fear of some future punishment. You see your happiness in expressing what you are, not in gaining approval or avoiding its loss./223

Laurence G. Boldt

How to Find the Work You Love

A Practical Guide to Creative Career Design
New York: Penguin Arkana, 1996
New Edition, 2004
(Quotes are from the Original Edition)

How to Find the Work You Love is a highly recommended career guide pocket option, for those who won't work through *Zen or the Art of Making a Living*. Now, when I say this, I have to justify it. I have worked two times through *Zen or the Art of Making a Living*, and yet did not find reading this smaller book boring. Why? The books serve different purposes. And this present book surely is not just a thinner copy of the larger career guide. No, it's an entirely different book.

Laurence G. Boldt is original in all his books. They contain each a specific message. What they have in common is the life philosophy, the underlying pattern as it were. It may put you off if you are a Christian fundamentalist. I once joined a Bible study group for the time of one year, and I did not know that the two men who were conducting it were fundamentalists. I only found out later, but I needed almost one entire year to get my senses together to really contradict them and finally, as they did not alleviate their judgmentalism for the slightest bit after my very explicit criticism, I quit. Now, I tell you that because I want to quote here what they said about Taoism, astrology and divination. You can put it in three dicta:

Published by Sirius-C Media Galaxy LLC, 2011

1) The Bible says that astrology comes from the devil. Therefore God has forbidden it.

2) Taoism is a fashionable new teaching of the devil. It teaches total irresponsibility.

3) Divining means cheating God. God has given us a rational mind for discrimination.

So, when you summarize their worldview, it means: all knowledge is forbidden, except what you can catch with your rational mind or left-brain. (Which means also that art belongs to hell, which is what one of the two men once mentioned to me in private conversation after the lesson).

Now, I put this squarely in your lap, because if you have this kind of mindset, please don't shun Mr. Boldt's books by applying your reductionism and your fundamentalist bias to them - because they have not merited such a treatment. They come as they are, with all the decoration, if you find it's a decoration, with all their embeddedness in a noble old and wistful tradition that we summarize today as Zen, while originally it was not a one-word tradition, so to speak, but a much more diverse happening. And diversity, yes, you have to embrace, if you want to understand Mr. Boldt's books, otherwise it's better you keep away.

Now, to begin with, Boldt stresses in this book that you burst your limits if you are at all serious about finding really meaningful work. Bursting your limits doesn't mean you have to become a superman or superwo-man, but rather means bursting your understanding of the world, and your humanness. It means accepting your soul-identity, and do away as much as you can with social conditioning. That in turn requires you to get in touch with inside and give priority to your inner world:

Laurence G. Boldt
At times it may seem that our inner world is nothing more than an endless chorus of conflicting voices. We hear them rattling around in our heads – the voices of the media and popular culture, the voices of our parents and peers, the voices of our escapist fantasies and infantile fears. To engage the creative life, you must be able to discern the voice of your own best self amidst the clamor and confusion of this strange and bewildering cacophony. You must be able to discriminate between what is really true for you and what merely sounds good./26

I have done this work from A to Z, over several years, and can testify for the validity of this statement. This is your turning point, this is, if you want, the test that God, if you are monotheist in your belief, has put up for you. It's really that hard, and Mr. Boldt did not joke when he said *bewildering cacophony*. It's not a movie that you can store away after having watched the drama of the hero. The movie reassures you because you know how the story ends, but in your own life as a potential hero, you don't know how it's going to end. When you read the Bible, do you get anywhere in this long tale the impression that life is easy? Then read the Koran, the Thora, and then the Vedas. In none of the scriptures you

Published by Sirius-C Media Galaxy LLC, 2011

are told that life is easy. So why do you believe it? You believe it because television tells you to believe it. And it's here where you are knocked out of your soul-being, like a ball that is kicked out of the football terrain, and lost somewhere in a street, where it has no more meaning. A football in a football field is a highly precious thing, isn't it? But on a beach, rolling along in a busy street, what is this thing, and why it's there? You see, all is connected, all is related, all is contextual, so to speak! And if you are not connected with yourself, with your ▶Self, with what are you going to be connected?

What Laurence G. Boldt says, and it's a meant to be serious, is that life while it's a game somehow is not an amusement, and that if you take it as an amusement, you are like the pack who go for everything just because everybody else does. If you are serious about your life and yourself, you will not take a job haphazardly, and you will do all you can to become clear about what you really want in life, and about what you want in your career. And to do this, you have to be honest with yourself. Boldt confesses:

> **Laurence G. Boldt**
> In my work as a career consultant, I have observed that men, especially, have difficulty admitting that their work life is not working for them. They endeavor to conform to the cultural stereotype of the macho man – the strong, silent type who has everything under control. They try to uphold the illusion that they have it all together, even though on the inside they may be falling apart. (This may be one reason why suicide rates are so

much higher for / men). Women generally seem more willing to acknowledge their pain. Among the men who seek my services, I see three general categories: young men or sensitive types who are not invested in the stereotype, those who come at the urging of their wives or lovers, or those who have already achieved considerable financial success. /35-36

You may think this is not the quick-fix career book you were searching for? Yes, right, it's not, and that's why it's a good book. After all, you can win a million in the casino, tomorrow night. And what are you going to do with the money? That's the big question. I have worked with a young Chinese in Rotterdam, Holland, once, and empowered him over six months. It was a test for me in my beginning career as a coach. I used all my tricks, so to speak, I just fired him up like hell. You know what happened? After about two years of constant intensive coaching, every day at least two hours, he won five million dollars in the lottery. And here we are, folks! What did he do with the money? Now, let me first ask, what did he do with *me?* He discarded me out of his life. Then he discarded his parents and his sister out of his life. He bought a villa in *The Hague*, in the quarter of the town where the Queen and Prince Bernard live. He wanted to be in that neighborhood, and nowhere else. Of course. He shut the door to me, his coach, he shut the door to his parents, and to his sister. Now, tell me, what do you think of this guy? And when you have thought deeply about him, I assure you, you are ahead of your generation!

Published by Sirius-C Media Galaxy LLC, 2011

Now, you may agree with me that this young Chinese lacked what we call human values. For him, to have enough cash in his pocket all the time was what he called *success*, and to have a villa near the Queen was what he called *prestige*. Now, is that what you want, success, prestige? This is the question all this book is about, or rather, all what this book is *not* about.

What touched me very deeply is what Boldt conveyed about his younger years, and how it came about that he embraced the career of a coach. He writes:

> **Laurence G. Boldt**
>
> In my youth, I spent a portion of my spare time visiting the elderly in nursing homes. I was struck, time and again, by how many of these people expressed regret about things they had always wanted to do with their lives, but hadn't. It wasn't just that they had failed to achieve their dreams: they had never even worked at them. Many had secretly cherished an idea of something they wanted to do for twenty or thirty years or more, but had never taken even the first step./76

Can you imagine? Can you see yourself there? My grandmother, the day before she died in a hospital without being really sick, at the age of seventy-three, said that all she did in her life was wrong. It had been a shock for me. My grandmother was the only person of the whole extended family I really always respected, and who taught me so much, and who had a noble attitude that contrasted very strongly with the attitude of her four children. Why did she say this? Later in life, through research on my family roots, I found the answer. She had a dream of something much greater than she had realized (and which was already great), but she had given up on that dream about twenty years before she died. And that is probably why she died and did not live twenty years or thirty years longer. What my grandmother said on her death bed was not true. She was the person I had most admired in my young life, and for whom I would have given a signed certificate to have done *everything right* in her life. But she saw herself differently. Why? Because she had much higher expectations of herself, and never had revealed these high expectations to us.

The lesson of this is that you have to *communicate* your expectations, without being afraid you are going to be ridiculed for your ambition. Life is a strange soup, our universe is a strange pudding, it's all about *communicating vision*. Yes. If you keep it inside, it's like a plant you put in a cellar and that can't really grow because it lacks sunshine. When you tell people what you want, and if it's the craziest idea in the world, you get that sunshine, even if they criticize it, then you get the sunshine in the form of anger, which is also a sun. But when you keep it inside, you bury it alive. And these elders, in the nursing homes, had done exactly that, they had buried their lives long before they themselves were buried. They had buried their dreams:

Laurence G. Boldt

The prevailing atmosphere of the nursing homes I visited was

Published by Sirius-C Media Galaxy LLC, 2011

one of profound sadness and regret. It was poignant to hear these people – many bedridden, some with trembling hands – tell their stories of regret./76

Now, this experience touched the young Boldt so much that he took something like a vow, dedicating his life to not only help himself avoiding the denial trap, but helping others to avoid it, too:

Laurence G. Boldt

Even more moving was / the emphatic way the urged me, with all the strength and force they could muster, to follow my own dreams, not to allow what had happened to them to happen to me. Had this occurred once or twice, it would have made a strong impression, but its repetition left an indelible mark. I learned more about how to live from these people than from all the books I had ever read or classes I had ever taken. At that point, I determined not only to follow my own dreams but to dedicate my life to helping others, in whatever way I could, to avoid the fate that had befallen these poor souls./77

And here I will stop this review, primarily for respecting the author, as extensive quoting would need the permission of both author and publisher, and second because I think it's good for you to stay on this moment of serious reflection about death, about old age, about things coming to an end, and taking this view as an inspiration for changing your life, changing your perspective of life, and changing your attitude. You have not a minute to waste, not a moment to lose, and not a second to chat just for passing your time. Your time should be dedicated to your mission - all the time! This is what this book and all books of career coach Boldt tells you. I wish to thank this great master of life for his teaching! It has deeply touched me, and hopefully it will touch you in the same way.

Published by Sirius-C Media Galaxy LLC, 2011

Laurence G. Boldt

The Tao of Abundance

Eight Ancient Principles for Abundant Living
New York: Penguin Arkana, 1999

The Tao of Abundance is in my view the best book that Boldt has written. It goes way beyond the stuff you would expect from a career coach, was he *only* a career coach. The miracle is that this man, contrary to many other coaches, is not just the leather of his wallet, and he is the only one in the illustrious world of life coaching for whom I would personally testify that his mission is his primer, not the revenues he makes from it.

This book is not a career guide, it's not a guide at all. It's the vision of a Bodhisattva. I believe Boldt has attained the spiritual level of a Bodhisattva, a spiritual guide. And this is what this book provides, *spiritual guidance*, nothing lesser than that. But not in the usual chewing-gum wrapping that you are used to when you expect somebody to talk about so-called spirituality.

Boldt will never obfuscate the message by rigidity of mind or of language, or by putting up inflexible strict rules. This is his unique genius. He is a very flexible-minded thinker and I sometimes wonder how an American can have such an Oriental mindset? But after all, we are universal souls, and from a certain point of spiritual evolution we are detached from all these labels, nationality, ethnicity, family pedigree, level of education, and such, and are just floating in space.

This book is written from the perspective of an accomplished master, if he calls himself a master or not, but he definitely is one! It is one of the most beautifully composed books I have ever had the privilege to read. But I admit that the book is not an easy read because of its complexity and integrated, holistic view of life. Why should we always want to understand a book on first read? I guess we have been conditioned to believe that well-written books have to be *easy to understand*. Is that so? Have you ever studied the Cabala? Is that easy to understand?

When I was reading Plato, Kant and Hegel at the age of ten, I found they were not easy to understand, and when I read them now, in my fifties, I still find them difficult to read. And I then discovered that the difficulty mainly comes from their particular point of view being different from mine. Then I tried to put myself wholly in their world, in their shoes, in their skin, trying to think from their perspective, and suddenly I found it was easy to understand what they were saying. So it seems my ego had been in the way, and thereby, my conditioning, my little opinions, my experiences, my way of looking at the world. To get to realize this, you actually step beyond your world, and when that happens, in that very moment, you forget about yourself, do what you will, and instead focus

Published by Sirius-C Media Galaxy LLC, 2011

on what the other is saying. By the same token, when you want to realize something that seems far beyond your present achievements and your present lifestyle, it is much easier to look into it, to imagine it, when you forget a little about your present world and your present me. This sounds very clear-cut, but it's not. It is a dialectic process. We are actually always with one foot in our future. Boldt elucidates:

> **Laurence G. Boldt**
> In the West, we have identified the ego as the final term of the self. The modern economic view of life, which pervades our culture, assumes the psychology of the ego, that is, the feeling of lack and the struggle for self-preservation. We have, more than any culture in human history, committed ourselves to the ego and its consciousness of lack. As a result, we are haunted by a prevailing sense of spiritual and psychological poverty in the midst of unprecedented material prosperity. We have elevated the ego to the status of a god and sought our happiness in its endless desires. Modern economic life demands the continuous expansion of these desires. Yet no matter how much we acquire, it never seems to be enough. We are never satisfied./xxviii

Of course, when you see your realization in material satisfaction, you can never be satisfied. Self-realization is not the shallow consumer credo that longs for material fulfillment. Work that is nourishment of your soul provides the endless streaming of love which is a fulfillment not easily put in words, but nonetheless real. This fulfillment comes from being aligned with purpose.

But you can't really cut off material abundance from the abundance of love. It's melted, but it's not synonymous either. But typically, the two go together, while one does not match out the other. Boldt writes:

> **Laurence G. Boldt**
> When we embrace our unique gifts and capacities as individuals and put them into expression, the road to true abundance opens before us./xxxiv

Now, what is abundance? Let us first ask what is *not* abundance, then it's easier to grasp what is abundance. What is not abundance, well, is what is all over the place. It's the mass mind, the herd instinct, the pack rule. It's the scarcity paradigm:

> **Laurence G. Boldt**
> The first task is to recognize the inner and outer forces that conspire to make us believe in scarcity and thus to feel lack. Awareness of these factors will help us to overcome their influence over us. The second task is to cultivate a spirit of abundance in our lives, celebrating the gift of life with joy and thanksgiving. As we focus on our thoughts and actions on things that bring a feeling of connection with all life, we begin to move with the flow of the Tao. In this way, we allow blessings to come to us as a part of the overflow of an abundant spirit – not as things we crave and struggle for from a sense of lack or desperation. To come from lack can only bring lack, even when we get what we think we need. On the other hand, when we come from the spirit of abundance, we attract ever greater abundance./13

Published by Sirius-C Media Galaxy LLC, 2011

There is a rather queer parable by Lao-Tzu that teaches us about what is essential in life and what is not, thereby conveying what brings abundance, and what brings decay:

Laurence G. Boldt
Lao Tzu reminds us that the useful part of the pot is not the outer rim that gives it form but the empty space within; the useful part of the house is the empty space within the walls, not the walls themselves./53

That's an incredibly smart observation. How can something be useful that does not exist or that is defined by its very contrary? Here you see how useful it is to get to grips with the obvious paradoxes of life, because they teach us long lessons about wistful living. But, as Krishnamurti pointed out, it's the same with love. We cannot define love, but we can well trace out negatively what is *not* love. While we cannot really describe what makes out loving behavior, we can easily enumerate patterns of non-loving behavior.

Abundance also means accepting your perverse behavior, because it comes from denial, and by accepting your upside-down energies, you accept that decision to deny parts of yourself, and to suppress certain longings. When you dissect your perverse love, you dissect all of your love.

Laurence G. Boldt
The classical Taoists take a much more positive view of human nature. For the Taoist, all depraved or perverse manifestations of

human behavior result from rejecting our deepest nature, not from following it. It is by denying the unity of all life and committing to the attachment of the ego that we go astray./97

And here, many of our young men and women today are stuck. They feel that some forms of their sexual behavior or at least their sexual desires, are perverse according to the quite limited standards of current society. And I have seen in the last ten years of my work as a coach that this inner conflict deeply affects their professional performance. To say that if you foster a rigid judgmental and moralistic paradigm, you will be at pains being professionally happy even if you deny yourself your perverse sexual wishes. This very denial, and this is the rub here, will have repercussions on your professional life. In the same way that you repress your allegedly perverse sexual behavior, in the same way you shall lack essential penetrative power (sic!) in your professional endeavors.

The way out? My answer is *Liberate your Minotaur*, which means to work on the denial pattern, so that your vital energies will flow again forward instead of backward. If you don't want to go this daring way, there are other options. Boldt, referring to William James, proposes to act as if, and thus to simulate the behavior pattern or role you would like to mold yourself into:

Laurence G. Boldt
The noted American philosopher and pioneer psychologist William James advocated the act-as-if principle as a powerful tool for transforming consciousness. According to James, it is easier

to act out your way into a new kind of thinking than to think yourself into a new way of acting. As you begin taking definite actions toward the accomplishment of your goals, you demonstrate to your subconscious mind that you are serious about attaining them. If you want to be a writer or a painter, begin writing or painting, even if you can do it only part time. The body of work you amass will convince your subconscious mind that you are indeed serious about your new career and on your way to manifesting it. (…) Dare to begin taking immediate action toward the results you see, and you get energy moving in that direction. You build a force of momentum toward the results you desire./114

The as-if method has proven very effective, for example, in pilot training. All pilot training is done by simulation, using a flight-simulator. This principle, you can apply to all of your life, because indeed you can simulate every possible situation in your mind, by using the power of your imagination.

I stop here because extensive quoting is not admitted under copyright law, and also because I think if you are really interested in this book you have to buy it and read it instead of just absorbing my own perspective of it, which despite my best intention is not how the author sees the world. And the real challenge for you is to face this message directly, by being exposed to the whole of its message. I have made my selections, my quotes, and you will do yours, and our quotes will not converge, as our lives, our experiences, our vision and our perceptions do not converge.

But I hope that you see that abundance is just that: an immeasurable wealth behind the little that can be measured. You can measure my book review by counting the words, but you can't measure the depth of this book when judging it by reading my book review. And this is why it's ultimately futile to write book reviews ...

Published by Sirius-C Media Galaxy LLC, 2011

TOM BUTLER-BOWDEN

Books Reviewed

50 Success Classics (2004)

Tom Butler- Bowden is a prolific young business author from Britain who has written and produced a series of highly successful books and audio books that are to be found in bookstores around the world. The book I am reviewing here, *50 Success Classics*, I found in a bookstore in Manila, Philippines.

The author has published similar titles, such as *50 Psychology Classics*, *50 Self-Help Classics, 50 Spiritual Classics*, or *50 Prosperity Classics*. These books are obviously manufactured from a concise concept that tries to condense highly interesting content and life experience for those who do not have the time or will to read the originals. The author is gifted with brilliant language skills, wit and a sense of humor that are truly inspiring.

Tom Butler-Bowden

50 Success Classics

Winning Wisdom for Work and Life
London: Nicholas Brealey Publishing, 2004

50 Success Classics is a highly useful book that surely has taken much work, as it's generally true that writing your own ideas is easier than correctly reporting the ideas of others in your own words. In this sense, the book has high value and is a precious asset in every business and personal growth library. Many of us won't have the time to read all the books and life stories reviewed by Tom Butler-Bowden, exciting, highly interesting life stories of highly successful, famous and extraordinary men and women. So much the more such a book comes in handy as it conveys the essential wisdom from fifty landmark books. This unabridged guide to the literature of prosperity and motivation surveys fifty of the all-time classics, giving you their key ideas, insights and applications—everything you need to know to start benefiting from these legendary works. From rags-to-riches stories of such entrepreneurs as Carnegie, Buffett and Walton, to master motivators like Zig Ziglar, Brian Tracy and Napoleon Hill, to such contemporary business blockbusters as Jack Welch, Spencer Johnson and Robert Kiyosaki, these are the leaders and pioneers who have helped generations of readers unleash their potential and discover the secrets of success.

Published by Sirius-C Media Galaxy LLC, 2010

Let me first point out what the author understands under *success*. It was very intelligent and thoughtful of his part to define what he means by that term as after newest stress-research, the term success itself has become controversial. This research namely found that especially in American society, success today is a trap for many, a surged-up high-voltage trip to the grave, a cosmetic and socially approved vintage of suicide that comes with a golden coffin! Heart disease, coronary, and colon cancer are its long-term laurels. It goes without saying that Tom Butler-Bowden does not talk about this kind of success, while it's the lot of most Americans today, and as a matter of cultural exportation, of many thousands of people every year worldwide, who in their confusion and their cultural alienation blindly follow the American business model and lifestyle.

So let me provide some quotes that indicate of what kind of success the author is talking in his book.

Tom Butler-Bowden

You need to make a distinction between a compulsion to succeed for the sake of winning, and the desire for enduring achievements that will enrich your life and the lives of others./2

Success requires a concentration of effort. Most people disperse their energies over too many things and so fail to be outstanding in anything./2

The greater part of genius is the years of effort invested to solve a problem or find the perfect expression of an idea. With hard work you acquire knowledge about yourself that idleness never reveals./3

Great achievers know that while the universe is built by atoms, success is built by minutes; they are masters when it comes to their use of time./3

Successful people have a good relationship with their unconscious or subconscious mind. They trust their intuition, and because intuitions are usually right, they seem to enjoy more luck than others./3

The greater the risk, the greater the potential success. Nothing ventured, nothing gained./3

These quotes show that the author talks about success that is wholesome to the person, that, while it entails hard work, is in accordance with the greater picture of our inner life, and especially our subconscious mind and our higher direction. It is by no means the compulsion-like success that many today take for the one and only form of social advancement.

By the same token, the author defines leadership as the ultimate form of expression, not a selfish power drive that needs to be acted out on the back on others. He writes:

Tom Butler-Bowden
True leaders are not interested in proving themselves; they want above all to be able to express themselves fully./19

Published by Sirius-C Media Galaxy LLC, 2010

Structured education and society often get in the way of leadership: What we need to know gets lost in what we are told we
should know./19

Real learning is the process of remembering what is important to
you, and becoming a leader is therefore the act of becoming
more and more your true self./19

Discussing Warren Bennis *On Becoming a Leader (1989)*, the author notes the following distinct criteria describing the know-how of becoming a leader:

Tom Butler-Bowden

- Continuous learning and never-dying curiosity.
- A compelling vision: leaders first define their reality (what they believe is possible), then set about managing their dream.
- Developing the ability to communicate that vision and inspire others to follow it.
- Tolerating uncertainty and taking on risk: a degree of daring.
- Personal integrity: self-knowledge, candor, maturity, welcoming criticism.
- Being a one-off, an original: Leaders learn from others, but are not made by others.
- Reinvention: to create new things sometimes involves recreating yourself. You may be influenced by your genes and environment, but leaders take all their influences and create something unique.
- Taking time off to think and reflect, which brings answers and produces resolutions.
- Passion for the promises of life: a belief in the best, for yourself and others.
- Seeing success in small, everyday increments and joys, not waiting years for the Big Success to arrive.
- Using the context of your life, rather than surrendering to it./20

The author explains that to lead, 'you have to make a declaration of independence against the estimation of others, the culture, the age', that you have 'to decide to live in the world, but outside existing conceptions of it', because '[l]eaders do not merely do well by the terms of their culture, they create new contexts, new things, new ways of doing and being'./21

And this kind of success also comes with certain obligations. It's not given for free. It has to be managed. Managing your success means, according to the author, that you manage your time, and your productivity. And it has to be incremental, one step at a time, but that step done safely, thoroughly and carefully. He writes:

> **Tom Butler-Bowden**
> Success may look fully formed when we behold it with the perspective of years, but those who have achieved it know that it arrived because they made every hour and every moment productive./27

> We are often so fearful of whether or not we can achieve something that we cannot see that if it is broken down into smaller, daily steps it becomes much easier./27

This kind of success also involves people management, both the people you are working with in a team, and the people who buy stuff from you. And, last not least, the people who are in the ring with you, and that you ought to consider not as your enemies but as your friends - because through their eyes, you can see your weaknesses. When you talk with customers, will you lavishly tear down your competitors, calling them imbeciles and cunning cheaters? The author sees success potential in the precisely opposite attitude, and he stresses values like optimism, friendliness, openness, and a positive attitude:

> **Tom Butler-Bowden**
>
> In contacts with clients, praise your competitors. It shows clients you are even-handed and won't hide anything from them./28
>
> When you greet someone, say their name./28
>
> For 30 days, smile frequently and watch it transform your life./28
>
> Don't ever engage another person in argument. Instead, ask questions whose answers are likely to bring them round to your viewpoint./28

Now, a very important point. Even the most ancient of authors in human business history when talking about good business and proper attitude stress the virtue of discipline and, on top of it, self-discipline. But what does this magic word mean? And how to apply it in leading people toward greater performance?

> **Tom Butler-Bowden**
>
> Discipline doesn't work with people who are not secure in what they are doing, only encouragement does. Praise gets them moving in the right direction. Though it need take up very little time, praise is the fuel that can drive a whole enterprise./32

Another value is what the author calls continuity, and what the I Ching discusses under the header of hexagram *32. Constancy*. What is the meaning of constancy, and what does it mean in business? The author illustrates this value in discussing Warren Buffett's stock management strategies.

Tom Butler-Bowden

What is most radical about Buffett is that once he chooses a stock, he hangs on to it. (…) Buffett had always craved, and had always felt enriched by, continuity: to work with the same people, to own the same stocks, to be in the same businesses. Hanging on was a metaphor for his life./52

Benjamin Graham said that one of the three important elements of a successful investor was firmness of character. Buffett has this in spades, because his style of investment has required him to stick to his convictions. As Lowenstein correctly notes, Buffett is so attractive because his value investing goes hand in hand with ideas like loyalty, integrity, and keeping things for a long time. These seem out of step with our era, yet they prove their worth in their results./54

Next, the author elucidates other values needed to build long-term success, such as focus, honesty, self-confidence, a set of positive beliefs and a basically rational mind that is able to evaluate reality with a minimum of what I call the pitfalls of perception. The author writes:

Tom Butler-Bowden

This is the power of focus, of sacrificing what you might gain by broadening in order to gain a smaller but well-defined market./58

Published by Sirius-C Media Galaxy LLC, 2010

Speaking comes from the heart, which is always true./59

If you exude self-confidence, people will naturally want to let you succeed. Self-doubt creates a perception of incompetence./63

What you believe about yourself, the world will believe about you./64

The higher level of black heart is reached when you are not driven by your shortcomings or emotions, taking action that is driven by your true spirit./64

If you like to present yourself as sugar-coated, you will lose out on any opportunities that may require you to seem sour or hardened./64

If you are a naturally negative thinker, make the most of it and don't try to adopt false positivity. Don't fall into the trap … of thinking / that you must change yourself before you will have success. You can succeed just the way you are./64-65

Another value or virtue of the successful entrepreneur has been called a sense of duty or fulfilling one's dharma.

Tom Butler-Bowden

At the personal level, dharma is the duty that is yours to fulfill in your lifetime. You cannot be a soldier and refuse to fight; you cannot be a doctor and refuse to operate. If you are a writer, you can't work in a bank. Once you commit yourself to your duty, the universe has a way of protecting you and freeing you from other worries./65

We were talking about managing time, but what is perhaps more diffi-cult, and yet a duty to fulfill for the successful business [wo]man is man-aging money. The author elucidates:

Tom Butler-Bowden

Although money itself is a mystery, whatever best expresses your brilliance will inevitably lead to wealth. It will free you from pov-erty and give you a mindset that attracts abundance./66

Money comes to those who save. Money multiplies for those who invest it. Money stays with the person who entrusts it to wise people. Money is lost when invested in things with which you are not familiar. Money is lost at a fast rate by pursuing get-rich-quick schemes./71

Although it seems obvious, the richest man in Babylon got that way because he lived within his means. In time, anyone who can live on 80 or 90 percent of their income can become rich./72

Last not least, the perhaps most powerful driving agent for success sim-ply is *desire!* But for making desire the motor of your success, you must know *what* you desire, what you want! That sounds simplistic, but it is really as simple as it sounds. When you are not clear about your true wishes, you may run for twenty years in the wrong direction, only to see afterwards that the effort was not worth it because all the riches you acquired on the way mean nothing to you - as it was not what you *really* desired. Discussing Robert Collier's *The Secret of the Ages (1926)*, the author explains:

Published by Sirius-C Media Galaxy LLC, 2010

Tom Butler-Bowden

Collier notes that once you have achieved, you are more likely to achieve again because you now have it in you to succeed. In a further analogy, he suggests that when you strongly desire something and believe that you will have it, it sets in motion a mental whirlpool that sucks in the things, people, and circumstances necessary to enable its realization. You develop a momentum that allows you to continue achieving but with less energy./76

The greatest discoveries, Collier notes, came from a person who actually noticed something everybody else had seen. The biggest fortunes, he says, were made out of opportunities that many had but only one person grasped. It is not that unsuccessful people never see opportunities; they do. But they differ from people who are called winners in that they rarely have the will or the courage to act on a good idea. They give themselves only the reasons why something could not be done, while the winner only thinks of how it could./76

Why is visualizing something you desire so important to its attainment? Everything made in the real world, Collier says, begins as an image. … By looking at these images several times a day, you prepare the way for their entry into your life. … There is an occult law that power flows from the higher to the lower potential, not the other way around. Therefore, always imagine the best possible outcome, and the forming of reality will follow this design./77

It may seem paradoxical, but few people know what they want. Humans may be a bundle of wishes and wants, but unless we hone these hankerings to a sharp point we will forever drift in a sea of unfulfillment./77

> The challenge is to refine our longings and discontents into a single powerful purpose. You begin this process … by making a list of everything you could possibly desire, then weeding out the things that won't serve you in the long run. If you're not sure which desires are best, ask, Will this tend to make me better, stronger, and more efficient?/77

> Once you have this sense of purpose, be willing to pay the price. Impose discipline on yourself and never let up on attaining your one true desire. Even if you are not brilliant, it does not matter in the long run, because the law of averages means that if you persist you will reap rewards./78

While my collection of quotes of this book was about ten times the size of what I put in this book review, I shall stop here for mere respect of the author's copyright. And anyway, knowing more about the book won't make it more attractive than it is. This book is brilliant in every respect, and I have great admiration for the relatively young author to have mastered such difficult a challenge. The price of the book, by the way, is very modest compared to what you get out of it.

Let me quote the author one last time, with a little side remark. I am working with Joseph Murphy's prayer technique since now about fifteen years, and Murphy stresses the more spiritual values that come a bit short in the present account of success values. But the author at least mentions one of them, a very important one: *gratitude*. Compared to spiritual values, the merely pragmatic values such as time management clearly glide into the background because they can be replaced. But

Published by Sirius-C Media Galaxy LLC, 2010

spiritual, eternal values cannot be replaced. A sense of gratitude is a thousand times stronger than the most excellent time management. One of the most powerful prayers, a prayer that actually brings about miracles, simply is 'Thank you Lord, for all the blessings I receive every day!'

Tom Butler-Bowden
Singularity of purpose can produced a relaxed knowing, a faith in your future triumph that all really successful people share. This sense of gratitude and knowing attracts what you want on the principle that like seeks like: things flow to the person who already appears to have./78

EDWARD DE BONO

Books Reviewed

The Use of Lateral Thinking (1967)

The Mechanism of Mind (1969)

Tactics (1991)

Serious Creativity (1992)

Sur/Petition (1992)

Edward de Bono is a thinking trainer, corporate consultant, writer and philosopher of worldwide renown that I do not need to present. His influence on business thinking and conceptual planning cannot be underestimated. He has been a freelance consultant for large corporations such as DuPont, Exxon, Shell, Ford, IBM, British Airways, Ciba-Geigy, Citibank, to name a few.

Edward de Bono has contrib-uted in a unique, outstanding and admirable way to the pro-gress of education, creative thinking and human resource development and,

more generally, the evolution of humanity. Unlike many corporate train-ing experts, de Bono was never restricted to this very special and in many ways very limited profession, but went way beyond, and is to be considered a true philosopher and conceptualist.

Edward de Bono's research on perception and the memory matrix of the human brain has had a decisive impact upon the formulation of some of my ideas on developing the human potential, about accelerated learning and whole-brain learning, as well as upon my concept of peak performance.

I found de Bono's books during the first years of my work as a corporate trainer in Jakarta, Indonesia, 1994-1998, and virtually devoured them. Shortly thereafter, as work notes for myself, I made a quote collection, and then wrote

SIX THINKING HATS
EDWARD DE BONO

the Edward de Bono Book Reviews. From the start, I integrated de Bono's Five Hats brainstorming technique as a game-like activity in my corporate training seminars.

I believe that de Bono is not only an excellent coach and corporate trainer, but much more than that: a philosopher and one of our greatest holistic thinkers, and one of the few people on earth who truly understand children. De Bono has created a new primary school curriculum that was adopted by the Government of Venezuela and implemented there as a revolutionary new form of effective learning in young age.

Edward de Bono

The Use of Lateral Thinking

New York: Penguin, 1967, reedited 1990

The Use of Lateral Thinking is one of de Bono's first publications, a book written in the 1960s, but it surely is one of his most important writings. It seems that few have understood the book when it appeared more than thirty years ago.

In the first chapter of the booklet, de Bono introduces the idea of lateral thinking and defines it as a concept that goes beyond creative thinking in that it encompasses the latter but covers a wider field. At the time when this book first appeared, de Bono's took wide-ranging conclusions from his research.

> **Edward de Bono**
> Orthodox education usually does nothing to encourage lateral thinking habits and positively inhibits them with the need to conform one's way through the successive examination hoops./15

It is interesting to know, in this context, that de Bono later submitted a draft for a new holistic curriculum of basic education to the Government of Venezuela. Not only in government circles, but primarily in business, de Bono is recognized as a leading and far-sighted coach and corporate trainer.

Published by Sirius-C Media Galaxy LLC, 2010

The second and third chapters of the book prepare the main part of the study which is represented by chapter four and unfolds as a meticulous examination of perception habits. In these preparative chapters, de Bono makes interesting remarks about how ideas are born. Where are ideas coming from? How to generate new ideas?

Truly, these questions are of primary importance not only for every artist or creator, but also for every company director and marketing department head. We could observe in recent years that it is surprisingly not always the large corporations but more often than not mid-sized or small companies that are leading the competition by their intelligent approach, focused customer care and an effective cycle of innovation. For de Bono, this was not new thirty years ago. He wrote that it is 'not possible to look in a different direction by looking harder in the same direction.' He thought that for innovation, the tough, will-powered, hard-working and typically Western approach is dysfunctional; de Bono rather adopts the Oriental paradigm of flexible intelligence as a major ingredient of long-term success.

One of the major tasks of lateral thinking, then, is to identify and over-come *dominant ideas* since a dominant idea can be an obstacle in the creative thinking process. In every business, dominant ideas are very subtly and often imperceptibly built into the system through the formulation of strategies, marketing slogans, habits and traditions, the archaic 'we have always done it that way and it has worked for us.'

In the fifth chapter, de Bono summarizes his thorough examination of thinking habits and traps and writes:

Edward de Bono

With most situations, what starts as a temporary and provisional manner of looking at them soon turns into the only possible way, especially if encouraged by success./68

In his book *Tactics* that I am also going to discuss in this book review, de Bono states that small or mid-sized success is often impeding grand and overwhelming success.

I can confirm de Bono's conclusions from my own experience as a corporate trainer and fully subscribe to the following quote:

Edward de Bono

The fluidity of a situation where nothing is rigid and everything is doubted all the time makes vertical thinkers extremely uncomfortable. Yet it is from this limitless potential of chaos that new ideas are formed by lateral thinking./79

It is known from the media that one of the world's most successful entrepreneurs, Bill Gates, consciously uses the chaos principle for spotting new business opportunities. With lateral thinking it is not necessary to be right all the time, writes the Bono.

Published by Sirius-C Media Galaxy LLC, 2010

Edward de Bono

Lateral thinking means getting down into the mud and searching around until a natural causeway is found./83

I recommend this well-written booklet to the young entrepreneur,

young being understood not as a matter of age, but as a metaphor for

inner preparedness and openness. Needless to add that for all those

who are, like me, in the business of coaching, this book is indispensable

in our private library.

Edward de Bono

The Mechanism of Mind

New York: Penguin, 1969, reedited 1990

The second of the five books I am reviewing is a booklet that develops and elaborates de Bono's original approach to creative thinking, as it was first exposed in *The Use of Lateral Thinking*. The book is quite unusual in that the author examines with scientific exactitude how our brain handles perception and how it processes information.

Using many examples for demonstrating his theory, Edward de Bono finally concludes that the specific memory surface that the brain uses for information processing is in itself a highly unreliable system. In Part II, 29: Overcoming the Limitations, de Bono writes:

> **Edward de Bono**
> The errors, faults and limitations of information-processing on the special memory-surface are inescapable because they follow directly from the nature of the organization of the surface./218

The only possible form of handling these problems, de Bono concludes, is the awareness that these 'faults' are inevitable, followed where possible by techniques that minimize the errors.

In the next four chapters of the study, Edward de Bono analyzes the process of thinking. He divides thinking into four categories, that are natural thinking, logical thinking, mathematical thinking and lateral thinking. He then discusses each of these modes of thinking.

Natural thinking that de Bono also calls simple or primitive thinking is characterized by being very fluent yet its very fluency is the source of its errors, to quote de Bono. This mode of thinking, de Bono says, is the natural way the memory surface behaves and its thought-flow is 'immediate, direct and basically adequate.'

Logical thinking is characterized as the management of NO, most logical processes being forms of binary equations of identity and non-identity. Logical thinking is seen by de Bono as a tremendous improvement of natural thinking, in spite of the limitations, that are pointed out in detail.

Mathematical thinking is held by de Bono as useful, however with the limitation that it is more adequate to describe things than people. Its greatest limitation is seen by de Bono in the fact that it is only a second stage system which is used to make the most of what has been chosen by the memory-surface in the first stage. Lateral thinking as a genuine mode of thinking has been developed by Edward de Bono himself.

Edward de Bono

The purpose of lateral thinking is to counteract both the errors and the limitations of the special memory-surface./236

De Bono makes clear that lateral thinking is  less concerned with information gathering than with information processing. In particular, he states that lateral thinking is more concerned with making the best possible use of the information that is already available on the surface.

Edward de Bono gives interesting examples to illustrate in which ways lateral thinking is essentially different from vertical thinking. To summarize, one could say that lateral thinking is a way of thinking that lets a door open for the unexpected to occur. With lateral thinking you may not know what you are looking for until after you have found it. There are several broad characteristics that show the obvious usefulness of lateral thinking, and Edward de Bono discusses them one after the other in his book:

– Seeking alternatives

– Thinking non-sequentially

– Undoing selection processes

– Shifting attention

– Giving random input

I do not need to further comment on this brilliant study which bears the stroke of hand of a genius. I guess that it was this book that laid the foundation for de Bono's overwhelming success as a thinking trainer and business philosopher later on. Strangely enough, then, that this booklet is the least known and perhaps the least popular among all de Bono books, but for one who is seriously interested in the foundations of lateral and of creative thinking, it is an absolute must-read.

Edward de Bono

Serious Creativity

Using the Power of Lateral Thinking to Create New Ideas
New York: Penguin, 1992, reprinted 1996

In *Serious Creativity*, Edward de Bono con-tinues the line of thought previously exhib-ited in *The Use of Lateral Thinking* and *The Mechanism of Mind*. However, *Serious Crea-tivity* is a much more elaborated study of lat-eral thinking in its broadest and most practical dimension.

The book consists of three major parts. In Part One, de Bono writes about the need for creative thinking and shows its theoretical and prac-tical applications. The author leaves no doubt about the fact that his approach is not primarily destined for artists and creators, but primarily for business people. Thus, not artistic creativity or inspirational creativity is the main application area of de Bono's approach to creativity: creativ-ity that we use to develop new and profitable ideas for marketing prod-ucts and for succeeding in the business world.

Accordingly, the style and the language of the book are ideally suited for entrepreneurs and executives, and it provides high practical value or, as Edward de Bono himself put it, it has take-away value. Interestingly, and unlike the two predecessors, lateral thinking is now only one element among others within the ten sub-chapters that throw different lights on the important question for every innovative company: how can we find and develop new and successful ideas?

Part Two is a very detailed and highly elaborated analysis of the use of lateral thinking in the brainstorming process.

From my personal perspective, I would like to add that the quality and the exclusiveness of the material presented here is such that it by far outreaches the competence of a creativity manager or innovation department. On the other hand, CEO's or corporate executive committees will seldom have the time and tranquil setting needed to digest the fantastic ideas and creative tools presented in this book, and to make the utmost profit out of it.

It is therefore important to emphasize what de Bono repeatedly suggests in his books, that is to create special *Concept R&D Departments* that are setup and trained for the unique purpose of providing new organizational and creative concepts for the creative growth and expansion of the company or corporation.

The material presented here is so vast that it by far surpasses the space to discuss it in a book review. This is so much more the case as de Bono has included his famous Six Thinking Hats brainstorming technique among sixteen other creative thinking techniques that are worth to be studied and tried out in practice.

From my own training experience I know that *Six Thinking Hats* is a topic vast enough to fill one whole seminar. I have been forced to include it as a secondary topic in my seminars because unfortunately in Asia creative thinking is not yet considered to be a primary topic for man-

agers. The result was that *Six Thinking Hats* was going to be the number one runner of all my corporate training seminars.

The detrimental effects of the traditional school system are such that every form of natural creative, independent and lateral thinking is as good as rooted out once we leave school.

The third part of the study is concerned with the practical application of creative thinking. This chapter is indispensable for every one who wants to setup training seminars or workshops on serious creativity. It is written in an exemplarily clear and practical as well as empirical style. Every little suggestion is useful in the day-to-day running of seminars or company workshops on creativity. Not to forget the Appendixes which are true jewels for the training practitioner:

Appendix One: Lateral Thinking Techniques;

Appendix Two: Use of Lateral Thinking Techniques;

Published by Sirius-C Media Galaxy LLC, 2010

Appendix Three: Harvesting Checklist;

Appendix Four: Treatment of Ideas Checklist.

To summarize, this book has more practical and direct-to-use value than its two predecessors which however have laid the theoretical foundation so that this book could come to existence.

De Bono's brilliant writing style and superiority in presenting sometimes highly complex content makes this book, among all other of the same author, a true enrichment of every business library.

Edward de Bono

Sur/Petition

Creating Value Monopolies when Everybody Else is
Merely Competing
New York: Fontana, 1992, HarperCollins, 1993

Edward de Bono's book *Sur/Petition* is very important. In my experience as an H.R. Consultant I can say that all the issues that Edward de Bono tackles in this extremely well-written book are still today hot issues, in the sense that they are unresolved so far in most businesses.

What is Sur/Petition? The basic subject matter of the book is the issue of creating value monopolies. Competing literally means struggling to-gether, whereas sur/peting, by contrast, means struggling ahead of oth-ers. How to get ahead of competitors?

The answer is by offering more value, integrated value, value that is yet unmatched by others and that, therefore, becomes a monopoly. As de Bono explains, value monopolies are not illegal forms of business con-duct because they serve the customer; they are specific solutions for the paradigm that Karl Albrecht called *Total Quality Service* or briefly TQS, as a parallel to *Total Quality Management* or TQM. This approach puts the customer first in the agenda, and not housekeeping or the company tradition.

Published by Sirius-C Media Galaxy LLC, 2010

Value monopolies can only be created after brainstorming has taken place which is based on a serious effort to understand and value the needs of the customer. It seems to me that presently large international companies are beginning to grasp the importance of giving the customer solutions that are of real and not only imaginative or marketing value. De Bono, as always, has looked into the future and offered solutions that most people, at the time of publishing the ideas, were not ripe to grasp.

The example that de Bono cites regarding *Ford* strikes. He had offered to Ford Britain to buy a company that owned large car parks all over Great Britain. He argued that cars are no more a lump of engineering and that a customer who buys a car wants and needs more, and more service in the first place. One of those needs being the urge to find a parking lot in town, de Bono's idea seemed brilliant. Now Ford could have connected a value to the existing value car which would have created a value monopoly. For de Bono's idea was precisely that at the entrance of those car parks a note would have been put that only Ford cars could enter them - and not other cars. However, Ford did not see the chance nor the need of their customers for more integrated value and did not realize the proposal.

Some years ago, the popular German car maker *Volkswagen* was brainstorming on the same lines and they found another brilliant solution.

They offered with selling a new car a bank account in their own newly created *Volkswagen Bank* as well as a free basic insurance for home and family. To make it round, third in the package was a special credit offer for new car customers.

Not only did Volkswagen sell more cars, the Volkswagen Bank surprisingly for many became one of the most successful and one of the most effectively managed banks in Germany, and this regardless of fact that at the opening of those banks, existing bank corporations were saying that Volkswagen as a car maker could never have the expertise and experience in doing effective banking. Needless to say that Volkswagen besides getting the right collaboration to have the necessary expertise in banking, marketed their concept so successfully now major banks in Germany see the Volkswagen bank as a hard-to-beat competitor - or should I say sur/petitor?

Mercedes-Benz and BMW developed similar surplus-value concepts and opened their Mercedes Bank and BMW Bank. What they give is even more. Every new customer, besides the afore-mentioned benefits, receives a credit card, with Mercedes-Benz even a one-year free-of-charge Gold Card that gives a whole range of benefits, so numerous that it fills a little booklet. It is really impressive to see it and it fully confirms de Bono's predictions!

De Bono always questions traditional ways of doing and goes straight to the root of problems. In the first chapter that is entitled *What is Wrong with the Fundamentals?* he calls efficiency and problem solving mere maintenance procedures and concludes that only effective solutions can bring success in the long run. Today, most of the Fortune 500 companies have realized this and other of de Bono's early ideas, but when de

 Bono voiced these requirements twenty years ago, he was taken as a visionary with lacking sense for reality. As it is so often the case, in hindsight we see that de Bono had more sense of reality than all his contradictors since what he predicted so many years ago is business reality today!

Reading Sur/Petition, one gets a feeling that in most businesses, at least in the Western world, there is a desperate longing for more creativity whereas, at the same time, and of course paradoxically, creative thinking is rejected as illusion, waste of time, or

as something for artists but not for business people and similar non-sense. Intelligent ways of dealing with business, and effective solutions, in the past as today are the exception.

Even among Fortune 500 companies which are, as a group, the most likely to adopt strategies and fixes as de Bono suggests them, are not immune against old mis-takes. The high turndown rate among Fortune 500s is an indicator for this fact. It is not enough to just understand the principles and to set up planning committees. The art of management is to walk the talk one wants all in the company to apply.

My experience has shown me that in so many cases, company directors are well ready to follow the advice of con-sultants but they think that they themselves were all perfect and the advice they get from their consultants usually is directed only toward subordinates. Whereas the truth is just that, in the contrary, *the boss has to adopt the new attitude first and thoroughly walk it through* before he can even expect others to ponder it for them-selves. This is the main obstacle of consultancy in the West, whereas in the Japanese business culture, saying something like that, I would voice a commonplace.

Published by Sirius-C Media Galaxy LLC, 2010

This book provides such an abundant source of wisdom and experience that it is almost impossible to review it. I am very inclined to say that nobody, and I mean this, nobody who wants to succeed in today's highly competitive world markets can afford to *not* read this book. Interestingly, when we study highly successful entrepreneurs and CEO's,

 we see that they intuitively apply the principles de Bono erects in this book and others he has written on this subject. I would like to cite Bill Gates as an example; his extraordinary success is not chance and it is not luck nor is it that he was trained by a business consultant like Edward de Bono. What I found after having studied various sources about him as well as from information received from people closely working with him is that he exactly applies all these principles in his management – and more. Gates goes even beyond. He is one of the few entrepreneurs who voluntarily apply *chaos principles* in their management to get out of the linear movement and into cyclic movements that are much more productive. What is perhaps the final secret for the success of every business leader or even every leader, it is the combination of business competence (the hardware) and people competence (the software). What Microsoft has done to get out of the claws of its competition, and sur/pete was:

- Creating value monopolies based upon precise knowledge regarding to what the mass customer expects and needs;

- Intelligent concept design that gives a familiar look to all Microsoft software;

- Superior striving for providing the utmost user-friendliness, intuitive handling and ease-of-use;

- Very conscious and careful approach in customer care and follow-up;

- Leading position in advancing new technologies, and courage and expertise to do so;

- High goal to bring out the most user-friendly OS ever known in computer history;

- Most advanced approach for people care one can imagine;

- Very careful examination of what the competition is doing for quickly and often boldly sur/peting it.

Value monopolies namely begin with pro-viding value and with valuing both the customer and oneself. The latter if often forgotten. A company that does not value their own achievements and strength, and  their staff, that has a low group self-esteem, will never brilliantly suc-ceed. However, high self-esteem, as de Bono observed in his book, is in practice often replaced by complacency. Complacency, de Bono states, is such a destructive attitude that he devotes twelve pages, a whole subchapter, to its discussion. More than once, de Bono reports that both arrogance and complacency are what he found to be the two strongest impediments for the implementation of the new customer-focused management strategies.

By the way, Karl Albrecht, in his book *The Only Thing That Matters* says something very similar. My own experience as a consultant is not different. My observation was that it is often also a matter of structuring an organization. I used to give training to hotels managed by one of the world's largest hotel management groups: ACCOR. The general attitude that reigns in this organization is aggressive management with almost no regard for the individual managers and their creative ideas. What counts are numbers, not creative input by people. I know from several hotel directors working for this group that this organization generally disregards any form of creative change, while from a local perspective

many hotel managers do good in sur/ peting their local competitors. This

has been shown a viable strategy especially for crisis periods, and I have seen with the *Red Top Square Hotel* in Jakarta, Indonesia, the former *Radisson Jakarta*, that this really works. After the end of the Soeharto regime and the ensuing political and economic crisis, the hotel was very low in sales, and others even had to close for lack of business. However, the Australian management of the Radisson decided to cater to the local Chinese, and this is how they turned their Chinese restaurant into a gold mine. This was going to work out very well and compensated for

some of the losses. I have seen this concept working well in exactly the same way later with the *Intercontinental Hotel* in Phnom Penh, Cambodia. Of course, for this to happen, the general manager of a chain hotel must be empowered to become creative on his or her own, and not be just an executioner of orders 'from above'.

A very interesting part of the book, for those who are not yet familiar with value-based management is the chapter eight entitled *The Three Stages of Business*. These three stages are enumerated as -

Product Values

Competitive Values

Integrated Values

Now, in the Western industrialized world, we have clearly reached the third stage that de Bono characterizes as follows:

Edward de Bono
In the third stage, attention is on integrating into the complex

Published by Sirius-C Media Galaxy LLC, 2010

values of the customer and seeking to achieve sur/petition
through concept design./111

It is only logical that at the end of this thorough study, de Bono suggests to implement entire Concept R&D Departments, an idea that
seems to be ripe eventually to be carried out in practice. However, in
traditional business settings, as de Bono remarked, it is still considered
as a threat to empower employees and to set up think
tank groups. As long as business or government is managed like the military, and this was the traditional way
to manage large corporations and government agencies all over the
world, we will not be able to move into management and leadership
that is –

Team driven instead of person driven;

People driven instead of technology driven;

Progressive, effective and ecological;

Flexible and unbureaucratic.

One of the purposes of Edward de Bono's contributions was to help us move away from this old management paradigm, that has become archaic and non-effective, and implementing, on both small and large scale a new, effective, ecologic and people-driven business management paradigm that is based upon values and the virtue of satisfying value-driven customer needs.

To summarize, this book that is supposedly not one of the most well-known Bono books, is yet one of the best productions of the author. For all people concerned with management, it is one of the most original books on management success strategies that have ever been published. I would even go as far as saying that it is a must-read for everyone who is in some way involved in leading people into the postindustrial era.

At the time Bono wrote this brilliant book, most of his daring ideas were rejected by the leading mainstream management paradigm. The author's unquestioned reputation as the leading think-tank trainer did not change this fact, nor the fact that among his clients were large corporations such as IBM, Ciba-Geigy, DuPont and other great names. This

Published by Sirius-C Media Galaxy LLC, 2010

is the somewhat frustrating point of departure of the book in the author's own words:

Edward de Bono

Government needs thinking very badly but does surprisingly little of it. (...) Business handles the analytical side of thinking quite well. But there is a need for improvement in the constructive, creative, and conceptual side. In the future, this is the aspect of thinking that is going to be essential for success./XX

With his habitual lucidity, Edward de Bono shows the present discrepancy between a new paradigm of quality management and the emphasis on housekeeping that used to be the flaw of traditional management. In the end you have to provide values that customers want, writes de Bono in the Introduction.

We can only hope that both government and business leaders will eventually comprehend and implement de Bono's futuristic ideas so that the new business culture will be more customer-driven, more flexibly intelligent and more creative.

Edward de Bono

Tactics

The Art and Science of Success
London: Pilot Productions Ltd., 1985
Fontana, 1991
Harper & Collins, 1993

Edward de Bono's book *Tactics* is a thorough empirical study on the subject of success and the various factors that may contribute to a person experiencing success. Together with a team of researchers, fifty-five highly successful people from business, finance, sports, art and fashion were interviewed. The excerpts of these interviews together with the author's very original classification of success into various categories and subcategories make the core of this most unusual and highly readable book.

To be true, the book is a treasure. The information you get is among the most valuable you can obtain not only for your business career but for your life as a whole. Most of the people interviewed showed uncommon views, high originality, and a daring, non-conventional, high-spirited, intelligent and bold approach to life, an approach that is never, in this form, taught or encouraged in school or university.

Let me begin having a look at the main characteristics that the author found to be valid for success in life and business:

Published by Sirius-C Media Galaxy LLC, 2010

Creative style;

Energy, drive and direction;

Confidence and self-confidence;

Stamina and hard work;

Effectiveness;

Ruthlessness;

Ability to cope with failure;

Tactics.

These were found to be the positively stimulating factors of success. Interestingly, not only the positive stimulants such as power, money or self-image were found to be contributing to success but also negative stimulants such as anxiety. The latter view is most unusual. Especially the exponents of the positive thinking movement sometimes seem to suggest that a well-directed life is always or at least most of the time free of anxieties. However, very successful entrepreneurs such as Robert Holmes à Court speak another language. Let me cite a passage in which de Bono summarizes the findings collected from different interviews on the matter of anxiety:

Edward de Bono

It is interesting that with successful people the anxieties are propellant rather than retardant. The anxieties push the entrepreneur forward rather than hold him back. There does not seem to be a search for the easy way or for security as such./60

In the introduction, Edward de Bono cites several traditional positions that people have seen to play a major role in success, such as

Being lucky;

Being a little mad;

Being very talented;

Operating in a rapid growth field.

However, despite the fact each of these positions can be defended, which de Bono shows in detail, he summarizes that there are complex constellations of factors and characteristics which the reader is entitled to assemble in any way he or she wants.

For everyone who is interested or practices astrology in a serious manner, it is a well-known fact that two persons with very similar astrological constellations can show very different ways of how they have realized the potentialities that their birth charts reveal. Therefore, initiative, drive and a sense for action at the right time and place is decisive for success in whatever field or profession.

As de Bono says, action does also encompass any kind of preparative action such as reading his book. A very important part of the study

Published by Sirius-C Media Galaxy LLC, 2010

deals with ideas and the question in which way ideas are relevant for practice and for successful action. Let's see what one of the interviewees, Lord Grade, has to say on this subject:

> **Lord Grade**
> The ideas you want are real ideas; they're not fantasies. There is a difference. The real ideas can be put into action. They are not dreams; they're something real. And what gets the team confident is that the entire team, the whole company, is successful./38

The question of style emerges boldly in this study. De Bono makes the interesting observation that changing one's personal style and imitating somebody else's style is not a success formula. This should perhaps be noted by trainers such as Anthony Robbins whose approach is subscribed to role modeling, a technique that in a way consists of modeling the style of some other successful person. In my own experience, this approach works indeed, and is quite powerful, but to the detriment of the self. It alienates people from their original self instead of bringing them personal fulfillment through being aligned with their soul level. Thus, it might well lead to worldly success, but at the price, for most people, to lose their soul.

De Bono states that the best way is to polish and somehow upgrade one's style, even though it may be a style that few people possess. In a paragraph entitled *Characteristics of Typically Successful Styles*, de Bono gives examples for energy, drive and direction as being one successful style among many. Let us see what David Mahoney who was named in Fortune Magazine as one of the ten toughest bosses in America, has to say about this subject:

David Mahoney

I just keep moving every day as hard and fast as I can. High-intensity and high-voltage. Light comes from that, not from passivity. I insist we all do our best every day. I'm intense in everything I do and I expect others will be, too. There may be timing factors in it, good luck and fortune factors, but the question is, do you utilize it? Some of it you can't control - some of it goes against you - it works both ways. You run to daylight - where you see the break you go. Most people aren't even aware of what's happening around them. Two-thirds of the people don't know what's going on to them, personally./39

There are of course other styles, such as the creative and inspiring style of Alex Kroll, president of the world's largest advertising agency, who transforms every challenge into a game-like setting that is inspiring himself and his staff for finding creative solutions out of playing around with the factors and parameters involved in a complex business situation. In addition, there are the managerial and the entrepreneurial styles. The question is if ego-based styles or can-do are original styles or if they are just attributes to other styles?

Chris Bonington who climbed Annapurna II, the Eiger North Wall, Kangur, Ogre, Annapurna South Face, and South-West Face of Everest says that it's also the great drive to find something in yourself, or a curiosity of finding whether this can be done. In the self-assessment program that is part of my own personal growth workshops, I have found that I am myself primarily motivated by this subtle curiosity.

The questions if one can achieve something daring and difficult are constant mirrors in every ambitious person's daily life, not only in my own life. There is no security in this, no conviction. There is only *intuition*. This intuition can however be very strong, as in the case of Paul McCready who incarnates the Can-Do style or attitude. This man made the first plane to fly using muscle power on its own, without any motor device, and he says:

Paul McCready
I went single-mindedly and with considerable assurance towards the goal./41

Nolan Bushnell, who created the billion-dollar video game industry and who was worth $70 million after the first decade of running a company with a $500 investment, says that he always feels like there is a solution. There we are indeed in the realm of feeling, of sixth sense, of intuition, and not any more in the realm of rational and calm planning.

Another style or style element is self-confidence and a certain amount of conceit. Roy Cohn, described by Esquire Magazine as a legal executioner … the toughest, meanest, vilest and one of the most brilliant lawyers in America says:

Roy Cohn

You also have to have a certain amount of conceit, which leads
you to believe that you and you alone can get things moving./42

In this chapter, de Bono examines all these possible styles and gives examples out of the abundant material that the interviews provided to
this purpose. At the end, he summarizes that as a preliminary condition
for success one should find out for sure about one's personal style and
maintain and develop it, building one's strong points rather than trying
to alter one's weak points, tracking every single decision or choice for
compliance with one's style, choosing the circumstances that best fit
one's style and, in addition being bold and egocentric, using failure as
the shadow that gives dimension to the picture:

Edward de Bono

An inflated balloon is vulnerable, but that is the only way it is
going to fly./57

The following chapters of the book deal with what stimulates success,
and what are the factors that may subtly influence success from child-
hood. Part II of the book teaches how to prepare for success and Part III
points out seven practical factors that are important to practice for everyone who sets out to be successful. These seven factors are:

Strategy;

Decision-making;

Opportunity;

Risk;

Strategy for people as resources;

Tactical play.

I can only express my admiration for this careful and precious study that has enriched my life in an extraordinary way. Every time I read again chapters from this book, it reveals me new insights, horizons and hints for my life, and in addition lets me participate in the lives of highly successful people.

SERGIO ZYMAN

Books Reviewed

The End of Marketing as We Know It (2000)

Sergio Zyman has been a leading figure, at times chief executive officer, at times marketing guru, with Coca-Cola, PepsiCo and Procter & Gamble. He is best known as the marketer behind *New Coke,* labeled by Forbes Magazine as *the most disastrous product launch since the Edsel.*

However Zyman and the marketing team at Coke did not adequately consider consumer loyalty to *Classic Coke* resulting in a major public relations failure. Since then Zyman launched a consulting firm called the Zyman Group that he sold to MDC Partners Inc., a Canadian investment company. Sergio Zyman has written four books to date on his experiences in marketing and advertising. (Wikipedia)

I am not a Coke addict, nor do I understand much of marketing, but that's exactly why I came to read this book, and did not regret it. In the contrary, I would read it once again had I not lost it. Reading this book was a great learning experience, a door opener, so to speak.

And I keep recommending this book to various kinds of people for we all need to know a little more from the thunder box of real life, of how making things happen in this world. To sell a black soup with the gigantic unrivaled success Coca Cola does since decades is something that, even if you don't like it, even if it doesn't quite fit in your new age or new spirituality worldview, you have to respect. We don't need to be driven by those realities, but we have to look behind their screens, to learn what the actors are doing when they are not observed. This is just an extension of school …

Sergio Zyman

The End of Marketing as We Know It

New York: Harper & Collins, 2000

The End of Marketing as We Know It is a highly interesting book, even if you are not a marketing man. This is so because you can learn a lot from the wisdom expressed in this book - because it's the wisdom of the world. I mean it's the wisdom of being successful in this world, in this postmodern international consumer world, where marketing has become so tremendously important. And you get insights as you can't get them from the media, while everybody today thinks he can write his little essay about marketing. Not so. What you get in this book is first-hand stuff that you won't find elsewhere. This is so because Zyman does not convey school knowledge, but personal experience, and personal experience he has got, and this almost everybody knows, as a former CEO and marketing man of Coca Cola. For Zyman, *positioning* is one of the most important rules in marketing. He early recognized the power of the competition, which means Pepsi, and then properly positioned Coke against Pepsi.

Sergio Zyman

While Coke stands for continuity and stability, Pepsi on the other hand, does stand for choice and change. Its positioning has al-

Published by Sirius-C Media Galaxy LLC, 2011

ways been about youth, doing things differently and unpre-
dictably. Pepsi is the insurgent, not the incumbent, but this has
its limitations as well. For Coke, a sentimental ad about going to
a family reunion and warm fuzzy images of Santa Claus drinking
Coke might be perfect, whereas for Pepsi drinkers, ads like this
would be a major shock. Managing these limitations is very
critical./86

Some of my friends asked me why I was reading such a book as it would
not fit in my 'otherwise new age and new science orientation'. Well, I
must admit that I don't care about those labels and distinctions. I was
always bad in marketing, all my life, and have rarely understood a bit of
the economics lectures I had to join as a law student during the first se-
mester law school. Zyman's book captivated me, and this was truly the
first time in my life that anything pertaining to economics and marketing could get my attention. Actually, as a result of reading this book, I
began to develop an interest in marketing, a matter that before I used to
dismiss and brush off the table as *pure manipulation*.

Well, when you read this book you won't probably unlearn that marketing is manipulation, but you will learn that it's a *science of manipulation*,
and not just random manipulation, and that even if you have a highly
successful brand such as Coca Cola and you are not strong in this science, you are soon out of business. But on the other hand, if you have a
bad product, the best marketing can't remedy that and you won't win
the sales Olympics, and this shows that marketing is *not only* manipula-

tion. If it was, you could sell just everything if only you cheat enough, and this is not what the market and life experience tell us. Consider what this man says, for he says it better than I could ever express it:

Sergio Zyman

I have succeeded in the marketing business not because I was just playing around, or because I had great artistic intuition. I have succeeded because I understand that it is business. I have approached every new campaign, every new promotion, and every product as an investment that has to pay a return. A profit producing business./6

In fact, the strongest point Zyman makes in this book is that marketing is not an art, not a creative muse where people engage in for fashionable reasons, but that every dollar invested in marketing must return through sales. Zyman writes:

Sergio Zyman

The truth is that, if you want to, you can measure the return on just about every dollar you invest in marketing the same way you can measure the return on a bottling plant or a new truck./7

When marketers understand that the goal is selling and not just running promotions, they sell a lot more stuff./12

The next point that Zyman stresses in his book is *strategy*. But he defines strategy differently as many other business people when they talk about strategic thinking in business:

Sergio Zyman

Strategic thinking is one of those terms that people use a lot to

And my friends who found this book did not fit in my new science library, are short-eyed, and may think that marketing gurus disdain a
deeper look into the thunder box. They ignore that marketing people
are those in modern society who take psychology for granted! They are
those who work every day with the principles that rule our subconscious mind, because publicity works that way. This is a simple fact, but
often overlooked. And then we talk about success. And Zyman writes:

Sergio Zyman
Put another way: it you want to be successful, / then you must
clearly define, in detail, what success looks like. Then you've got
to figure out how to get there./26-27

This quote seems to be taken from a book about new spirituality that
gives precise instructions about how to make a wheel of fortune or how
to define all the things you wish to receive from life. Because that's exactly what those books tell you: that success is just a word and that you
have to fill that word with meaning, the meaning success has for you.

Some life coaches even add that you have to express it in precise numbers, like 'I am going to have one million dollars in one year from now'.

Debriefing is a very important notion in Zyman's marketing vocabulary. He says you have to debrief both success and failure, and then adds:

Sergio Zyman

One reason to debrief success is obviously to figure out what is working and why, so that you can replicate the success in other circumstances. But there is another reason to debrief success. Don't be blinded by your assumptions. Just because you run a promotion and it works doesn't mean that it worked for the reasons that you thought it would./51

Zyman has many original ideas that you won't find expressed, at least not in that high condensation, in any university lesson about marketing. For example, he writes about incremental marketing versus horizontal marketing:

Sergio Zyman

Incremental marketing is much cheaper than horizontal marketing. You can spend less and sell more. You still have to spend on refreshing your brands, reminding people why they like your stuff, and giving them more reasons to buy it. If you want people to buy your product every day, you have to market every day, and if you want them to buy more, you have to give them more reasons. But it is much more efficient to build relationships with consumers and then work on getting the people who know you to buy more stuff than it is to go out and find new customers every day./69

Published by Sirius-C Media Galaxy LLC, 2011

Zyman warns repeatedly about complacency and the need to challenge your own product over and over, and I think he has walked his talk here when he was working for Coca Cola, and part of his success was to challenge the good with the better:

Sergio Zyman

You need to constantly challenge your own concept, even if you are proud of what you have created, even if it seems original, even if on the surface it looks like something totally proprietary. You have to make sure that it is indeed proprietary and remains that way, and that you can go up against your competitors day in and day out by defining and redefining yourself, and them, in unequivocal terms./74

Now, as I won't abuse with quoting from copyrighted material, I will supply just two more quotes for showing that this book is not a theory manual on marketing but gives very valuable and practical advice. I will provide two examples. The first quote regards portfolio management:

Sergio Zyman

Portfolio management says that you create artificial categories for each of your products and you don't let any of them cross over into the others. Why? To avoid cannibalizing your own customer base. That's a great idea, and while drawing these faint lines in the sand sounds nice in theory, in the real world, things aren't so neat and tidy. Somebody is going to compete with your products and try to steal your customers. If someone's going to do it, why shouldn't it be you?/75

I suppose that creating the *Sprite* brand was cannibalizing indeed Coke's customer base, but at the same time it was an expansion of sales as instead of one portfolio you got two afterwards, and the impact on the competition might have been confusing, to say the least. The second quote shows the pitfalls of portfolio management if your core product is weak, and this may explain why it worked in the Coke-Sprite case, because Coke was indeed a strong product:

Sergio Zyman

Go simultaneous, don't go sequential. And it's okay to cannibalize your own brand, because it's better to eat your own babies than have a competitor do it. If for any reason your core brand has a weak spot and another brand is likely to take volume from that brand, you better go fix your core brand. Don't try to fix your problem by artificially protecting your core brand with portfolio management. Deal with your competition, internally and externally, by being competitive! After all, it's much better to lose volume to yourself than to your competitor./76

I think this suffices to show that this book is somehow invaluable, that it has no equal because it's not a text book on marketing, but rather a text book on going beyond marketing. You have to read it all, from the first to the last page, to understand what the author means because it's not taken for granted to put decades of day-to-day experience in a book; that means in fact that the author has done a major work of compression, of condensing the input to some kind of essence. You get the feel when you read these quotes, and read them again and again. There is much more to it, and probably, if you are yourself a marketing person, you should expand from the book and do your own research on Coke,

Published by Sirius-C Media Galaxy LLC, 2011

on Sprite, or even on competitor Pepsi and all the other important details the Zyman mentions in his book.

I regret to not have found this book earlier in my life for I would not have run around for so many years of my life as a marketing idiot! But of course, for me, as a 'university guy' and academic, I have to do further studies, but this book gives me the motivation to sustain my quest - and this is a good thing to happen.

Generally, what I learnt from this experience is something Dale Carnegie taught in his seminars. He used to say that if you want to be successful, you have to learn seeing things from more than one perspective, and the one single thing or habit to get there is to read just about any kind of book, and this as an ongoing exercise your life through. In fact, I would never have considered buying such a kind of book if not, by a magic stroke of destiny, and on a business trip, eventually relaxed and open-minded, I had seen the well-designed cover in that airport bookstore in Singapore. And still relaxed, and at that moment not considering my usual interests, I was just reading one or two pages. What captivated me at once was the *language* of the author, his way to express things in a very distinct and precise manner that had something almost amusing about it. I found it refreshing that this book was *not* academic and that it was *not* new age or new science, and that it was, perhaps deliberately so, *not* spiritual. I am convinced it's good to read this book as a wake-up call when you are on your next new age trip, or your next spiri-

tual trip, courting the danger to lose ground with everyday reality …

Published by Sirius-C Media Galaxy LLC, 2011

Bibliography

Boldt, Laurence G., *Zen and the Art of Making a Living, A Practical Guide to Creative Career Design*, New York: Penguin Arkana, 1993, New and Updated Edition, 1999

Boldt, Laurence G., *How to Find the Work You Love, A Practical Guide to Creative Career Design*, New York: Penguin Arkana, 1996

New Edition, 2004

Boldt, Laurence G., *The Tao of Abundance, Eight Ancient Principles for Abundant Living*, New York: Penguin Arkana, 1999

Tom Butler-Bowden, *50 Success Classics: Winning Wisdom for Work and Life*, London: Nicholas Brealey Publishing, 2004

Edward de Bono, *The Use of Lateral Thinking*, New York: Penguin, 1967, reedited 1990

Edward de Bono, *The Mechanism of Mind*, New York: Penguin, 1969, reedited 1990

Edward de Bono, *Serious Creativity, Using the Power of Lateral Thinking to Create New Ideas*, New York: Penguin, 1992, reprinted 1996

Edward de Bono, *Sur/Petition, Creating Value Monopolies when Everybody Else is Merely Competing*, New York: Fontana, 1992, HarperCollins, 1993

Edward de Bono, *Tactics, The Art and Science of Success*, London: Pilot Productions Ltd., 1985, Fontana, 1991, Harper & Collins, 1993

Sergio Zyman, *The End of Marketing as We Know It*, New York: Harper & Collins, 2000

Published by Sirius-C Media Galaxy LLC, 2011

FROM THE SAME AUTHOR

A Bibliography

You can search publications from here:
http://ipublica.com/books/

For audio books and music, you can start here:
http://ipublica.com/audio/

All paperbacks, audio downloads, audio book compact discs, music downloads and music compact discs as well as Kindle books are referenced on the site.

For free podcasts search iTunes under my author name.

For quoting any of my publications, please use the following form:
Pierre F. Walter, [Title]: [Subtitle], Newark: Sirius–C Media Galaxy LLC, 2011

Web Presence

Pierre F. Walter on the Web

Sites

http://authoryourlife.com

http://ipublica.com

http://ipublica.net

http://ipublica.org

http://ipublica.tv

Video Channels

http://youtube.com/user/ipublica

http://youtube.com/user/authoryourlife

http://vimeo.com/pierrefwalter/channels

http://ipublica.blip.tv/

http://authoryourlife.blip.tv/

http://emosexuality.blip.tv/

http://pierrefwalter.blip.tv/

Published by Sirius-C Media Galaxy LLC, 2010

www.ingramcontent.com/pod-product-compliance
Lightning Source LLC
Chambersburg PA
CBHW081548170526
45166CB00009B/2621

* 9 7 8 1 4 6 8 1 4 5 1 2 0 *